WHO'S WHO
IN THE BIBLE
MADE EASY

ROSE
PUBLISHING

Who's Who in the Bible Made Easy
Copyright © 2023 Rose Publishing

Published by Rose Publishing
An imprint of Tyndale House Ministries
Carol Stream, Illinois
www.hendricksonrose.com

The *Made Easy* series is a collection of concise, pocket-sized books that summarize key biblical teachings and provide clear, user-friendly explanations to common questions about the Christian faith. Find more *Made Easy* books at www.hendricksonrose.com.

ISBN 978-1-4964-7807-8

Cover and layout design by Cristalle Kishi

Some photos and illustrations used under license from Shutterstock.com. Image on p. 53 copyright © 1989 by Joan Pelaez. Mosaic on p. 64 by Radbod Commandeur (1890–1955); photograph by Deror avi/Wikimedia Commons. Image on p. 68 by Donald Kueker, copyright © 1989 by Tyndale House Publishers.

Printed in the United States of America
010323VP

AARON

Aaron was the brother of Moses and Miriam. God gave Aaron the task of being Moses's assistant. Moses thought he was a clumsy speaker, so God allowed Aaron to speak for him. Together they went to Pharaoh and asked Pharaoh to let the Israelites go. When Pharaoh refused, Moses and Aaron performed signs and wonders from God.

After the Israelites escaped from Egypt, God appointed Aaron as the first high priest of Israel. He supervised the priests and the activities of the tabernacle. God also made a law that all high priests after Aaron must be one of Aaron's descendants. Despite these honors, Aaron committed a terrible sin. When Moses was meeting with God on Mount Sinai, the Israelites grew impatient for Moses to return. They urged Aaron to build a golden calf idol to lead them, and Aaron agreed. Aaron was not allowed to enter the promised land and died in the wilderness.

Ex. 7:1–6; 16:1–6; 28:1–2; 32:1–35; Num. 3:10; 20:22–29

ABIATHAR

Abiathar was a priest who served at Nob. King Saul ordered the death of the priests who served there because they had helped David escape from Saul. Abiathar was the only survivor. He fled to join David and told him the news. Much later, Abiathar betrayed David by supporting Adonijah's attempt to inherit David's throne. When Solomon became king, he removed Abiathar from the priesthood.

1 Sam. 22:6–20; 1 Kings 1:5–7; 2:23–27

ABIGAIL

Abigail was the wife of Nabal. Nabal did not treat David and his men well while they were running from Saul. Abigail went to David with gifts of food and begged for forgiveness. She counseled him to act in the kingly manner God had called him to instead of taking revenge. Not long after, Nabal died, so David married Abigail.

1 Sam. 25:1–42; 2 Sam. 3:2–3

ABIHU AND NADAB

Abihu and Nadab were sons of Aaron, the first high priest. They offered "unauthorized fire" to the Lord while serving in the tabernacle during Israel's wilderness wanderings. As a result, fire from the Lord consumed and killed them. This incident set an example for God's standard of holiness.

Lev. 10:1–2

ABIMELEK, PHILISTINE KING

Abimelek is a title for kings who ruled in Philistia. When Abraham and Sarah lived there, Abimelek took Sarah into his palace because she was so beautiful. God quickly revealed that Sarah was married, and Abimelek released her. Later, these same events happened with Abraham's son Isaac and his wife Rebekah, although likely with a different Abimelek.

Gen. 20:1–18; 26:1–11

ABIMELEK, SON OF GIDEON

This Abimelek was a son of Gideon, the famous judge in Israel. He tried to gain power by murdering all seventy of his brothers so he alone would rule over Shechem. He convinced the people to declare him king, then halted a rebellion by slaughtering them. When Abimelek attacked another city, a woman dropped a millstone on his head. Abimelek knew he would not survive, so he asked his armor bearer to kill him with a sword.

Judg. 8:31–9:57

ABISHAG

A beautiful virgin, Abishag cared for King David in his old age. In an attempt to become king after David's death, one of David's sons asked to marry Abishag. According to ancient custom, this was equal to claiming the throne. King Solomon saw the request as a threat and had him killed.

1 Kings 1:1–4; 2:13–25

ABISHAI

Abishai was one of King David's bravest warriors and a nephew of David. He was also a brother of Joab and Asahel, important men in David's army. Abishai helped stop Absalom's rebellion and saved David's life in a battle with the Philistines. He was often vengeful and cruel, however. He wanted to kill King Saul, and he helped Joab kill one of their rivals.

1 Chron. 2:13–16; 1 Sam. 26:5–12; 2 Sam. 3:30; 18:2; 21:16–17; 23:18–19

ABNER

Abner was the commander of King Saul's army. After Saul died, Abner made King Saul's son the next king and continued to lead his army against King David's forces. Later, however, Abner changed sides and supported David. Joab, the commander of David's army, feared that Abner was being deceptive. He was also angry that Abner had killed his brother Asahel, so Joab murdered Abner. King David mourned greatly for Abner.

1 Sam. 14:50; 2 Sam. 2:8–32; 3:6–39

ABRAHAM

Abraham and his wife, Sarah, obeyed when God asked them to leave their home and family and travel to Canaan. God promised Abraham many descendants who would inherit that land. Because Abraham believed God, God considered him righteous. Sarah was childless and barren, so Abraham fathered a child through Sarah's servant. But later God revealed that his promise would be fulfilled through a son who would be born to Sarah. God was faithful, and Sarah gave birth to Isaac. Abraham traveled throughout Canaan, and the Lord blessed him with much wealth. After Sarah died, Abraham married and had other sons. God's promise to bless all nations through Abraham came to pass through Jesus Christ, who descended from Abraham.

Gen. 12:1–7; 13:2; 15:1–8; 16:1–17:22; 25:1–2; Matt. 1–17

ABSALOM

Absalom was a son of King David. He was handsome in appearance but rebellious in his heart. Absalom arranged for the death of his half-brother, who raped his sister, Tamar. Then Absalom fled Israel for three years. Absalom eventually returned, but David was still angry with him for what he had done. Absalom staged a rebellion to take over David's throne, and David and his advisers were forced to flee. David's troops eventually killed Absalom and crushed his army.

2 Sam 13:1–18:16

ACHAN

Achan took plunder from the battlefield when Israel had been instructed to not take anything. His disobedience caused Israel to lose an important battle against the

Canaanite city of Ai. Achan was stoned to death as punishment.

Josh. 7:1–26

ADAM

Adam was the first man God created. God formed him from dust and placed him in the garden of Eden to care for it. Adam also named the animals. None of them made a good helpmate, so God created Eve from one of Adam's ribs. She became his wife, and Adam and Eve enjoyed life in the garden and fellowship with God. When Adam disobeyed God and ate the forbidden fruit that Eve offered him, sin and death came into the world. God was grieved and punished Adam with painful earthly toil outside the garden. But God also promised to send a Redeemer. Jesus Christ is the new Adam who destroyed sin and death.

Gen. 2:4–3:24; 1 Cor. 15:45–49

ADONIJAH

This son of King David schemed to inherit the throne, which David had promised to Adonijah's half-brother Solomon. When the elderly David learned about it, he ensured that Solomon was quickly made the new king. Solomon was merciful to Adonijah at first. But when Adonijah made a new attempt for the throne, Solomon arranged for Adonijah's death.

2 Sam. 3:4; 1 Kings 1:1–2:25

AHAB, KING

Ahab, seventh king of the northern tribes of Israel, was more evil than any king who had come before him. He married a wicked woman named Jezebel, who led Israel to worship idols and killed God's prophets. Ahab died when he was wounded by an arrow in battle.

1 Kings 16:28–33; 18:4; 22:29–37

AHIMELEK

Ahimelek was a priest at Nob. David went to Ahimelek for supplies and guidance when he was fleeing from King Saul. Ahimelek gave David bread from the tabernacle and Goliath's sword. Saul's chief shepherd was there and reported what had happened. In revenge, Saul ordered the killing of eighty-five priests and everyone who lived in Nob.

1 Sam. 21:1–9; 22:6–20

AHITHOPHEL

He was David's trusted adviser who betrayed him by joining Absalom's rebellion. When Absalom rejected Ahithophel's advice, Ahithophel hanged himself in his hometown.

2 Sam. 15:12–37; 16:15–17:23

AMASA

Amasa was a nephew of King David. Amasa commanded Absalom's army when Absalom rebelled against David. But after Absalom was killed, David pardoned Amasa and made him commander of his own army in place of Joab. Not long after, Joab avenged this move by killing Amasa.

2 Sam. 17:25; 19:1–13

AMNON

Amnon, a son of King David, became obsessed with his half-sister, Tamar. He pretended to be sick and arranged for Tamar to serve him a meal in his room. He tried to convince her to sleep with him. When Tamar refused, he raped her. Two years later, Tamar's brother Absalom arranged for Amnon to be killed in revenge.

2 Sam. 13:1–33

AMOS

Amos, a farmer and shepherd, was called by God to be a prophet. He delivered a message of judgment to the Northern Kingdom of Israel. The people there had corrupted the worship of God, treated the poor and weak with injustice, and betrayed their vows to God. The result would be their destruction at the hands of a foreign nation. But Amos provided them with a glimmer of hope: God would make sure that a small group of Israel's people would return and remain there forever.

Amos 5:6; 9:15

ANANIAS AND SAPPHIRA

Ananias and his wife, Sapphira, were part of the early church in Jerusalem. They sold their possessions and gave part of the money to the apostles. However, they claimed they gave the apostles *all* the money they had gained. Through the Holy Spirit, the apostle Peter knew they were not telling the truth. When Peter accused them of lying, they each fell down dead.

Acts 5:1–11

ANANIAS OF DAMASCUS

Ananias was a Christian who lived in Damascus. He received a vision from the Lord telling him to find Saul. Saul, known today as the apostle Paul, was a Pharisee who did not believe Jesus was the Messiah. Saul was going to Damascus to persecute Christians. But on the way, he had a powerful encounter with Jesus that blinded him for a short time. God was trying to get Saul's attention, and it worked. Saul became a believer in Jesus Christ. Ananias went to the house where Saul was staying. There he healed Saul's blindness and urged him to be baptized.

Acts 9:1–19

ANANIAS THE HIGH PRIEST

Ananias was Judah's high priest during the early years of
the church. He was known for his cruelty. When the apostle
Paul was arrested in Jerusalem, Ananias ordered that he be
struck in the face. Paul responded by accusing Ananias of
being a hypocrite. Later, Ananias accused Paul in front of
the Roman governor Felix.

Acts 23:1–5; 24:1–21

ANDREW

Andrew was a fisherman and disciple of John the Baptist
before becoming a follower of Jesus. The first thing Andrew
did after meeting Jesus was to find his brother Simon Peter.
Andrew told him that Jesus was the Messiah, and Peter also
became a disciple. Later, when Jesus wanted to feed five
thousand people who had come to him for
healing, Andrew told Jesus about a boy
with a small lunch. Jesus multiplied this
small amount of food into enough for
the entire crowd.

Mark 1:16; John 1:40–42; 6:8

ANNA

Anna was a widow for more than
fifty years. She was a prophetess
and a devoted worshiper of God
who spent day and night at the
Jewish temple. When Jesus's

parents came to dedicate him to God at the temple, Anna recognized that the baby was Israel's promised Messiah.

Luke 2:36–38

ANNAS

Annas was a former Jewish high priest who was present at Jesus's trial. Annas was also among the Jewish leaders who warned the apostles John and Peter not to speak to the crowds about Jesus again.

Luke 3:2; John 18:12–13, 24; Acts 4:5–22

APOLLOS

Apollos was an educated Jew from Egypt. Aquila and Priscilla met Apollos in Ephesus, where he was preaching about Jesus. However, Apollos still did not fully understand the gospel message. Aquila and Priscilla filled in the gaps so his knowledge was complete. Apollos became a missionary and helped oversee the church in Corinth.

Acts 18:24–19:1

AQUILA AND PRISCILLA

These early Christians were tentmakers, like the apostle Paul. They traveled to Syria with Paul. When he left Ephesus, they stayed behind to minister in the church there. Eventually they shared the gospel with Apollos, who became an important leader in the church. Paul mentioned Aquila and Priscilla in some of his letters, indicating they remained important ministry partners.

Acts 18:1–3; 18–26; Rom. 16:3–5; 1 Cor. 16:19; 2 Tim. 4:19

ASA, KING

Asa, Judah's third king, pleased God by driving out idol worshipers from the land. During his reign, he fought the Cushites and made a treaty with Aram to protect Judah from King Baasha of Israel. He died of a severe foot disease.

1 Kings 15:8–24; 2 Chron. 14:1–16:14

ASAHEL

Asahel was a nephew of King David and a mighty warrior in David's army. Asahel was a fast runner. During a battle with King Saul's forces, Asahel pursued Abner, Saul's commander. Abner warned him to stop, but Asahel would not give up. Finally, Abner killed Asahel. Later, Abner suffered the same fate when Asahel's brothers took revenge and killed him.

2 Sam. 2:17–23; 3:22–30; 23:24

ASENATH

The daughter of an important Egyptian priest, Asenath was Joseph's wife. Their sons Manasseh and Ephraim became two of the tribes of Israel.

Gen. 41:45, 50–52

ASHER

Asher was the eighth son of Jacob. His mother was Zilpah, Leah's maidservant. His name means "happy."

Gen. 30:12–13

ATHALIAH, QUEEN

Athaliah became the seventh ruler of
Judah when her son, King Ahaziah,
died. She put to death her rivals
to the throne, but a few years
later she was killed by her army on
orders from the priest Jehoiada.

2 Kings 11:1–20; 2 Chron. 22:10–23:21

BALAAM AND BALAK

Balaam was a pagan prophet. Balak, a Moabite
king, hired Balaam to curse Israel. But God warned Balaam
that he was only allowed to bless Israel. Balaam eventually
led Israel to worship idols. When the New Testament was
written, Balaam was considered a prime example of a
person whose teachings should not be followed.

Num. 22:1–24:25; 2 Peter 2:15; Jude 1:11; Rev. 2:14

BARABBAS

He was a notorious criminal charged with robbery,
rebellion, and murder. The mob at Pilate's palace chose to
release him instead of Jesus.

Matt. 27:16–26

BARNABAS

Though his real name was Joseph, Jesus's apostles called
him Barnabas. His name means "son of encouragement."
Barnabas brought Saul of Tarsus to the apostles when

others refused to believe he had become a Christian. Barnabas and Saul/Paul spent a year serving the church in Syrian Antioch. After this, they went on a long journey together to spread the good news about Jesus.

Acts 4:36; 9:1–27; 11:22–26; 13:1–3

BARTHOLOMEW (NATHANAEL)

When the Gospels list Jesus's disciples, Bartholomew's name is always immediately after Philip's. Outside of these listings and the one in Acts 1:13, we do not see Bartholomew's name again in the New Testament. Since Philip is described as introducing a "Nathanael" to Jesus, many scholars believe Bartholomew and Nathanael were the same person.

Matt. 10:3; Mark 3:18; Luke 6:14; John 1:45–51; Acts 1:13

BARTIMAEUS

This blind beggar from Jericho called out for Jesus to have mercy on him. When the crowd criticized Bartimaeus, he only called out louder. Jesus declared to Bartimaeus that his faith had healed him, and immediately he could see.

Mark 10:46–52

BATHSHEBA

King David spied Uriah's beautiful wife, Bathsheba, bathing on a nearby rooftop. David lusted after her and had her brought to him. When Bathsheba became pregnant, David tried to protect himself by arranging for Uriah's death. David married Bathsheba who gave birth to their child, but he died soon afterward. Bathsheba later gave birth to Solomon, who was crowned king after David.

2 Sam. 11:1–27; 12:13–25; 1 Kings 1: 11–31

BEELZEBUL

This name means "lord of the flies" and was used to refer to Satan. Jesus's enemies called him Beelzebul in an attempt to discredit his power to drive demons out of people. They claimed his power came from Satan and not from God.

Mark 3:22–30

BELSHAZZAR

God gave this Babylonian king a strange vision of a hand writing on a wall. The prophet Daniel explained to Belshazzar the meaning of the message: Because Belshazzar was too proud, God would give his kingdom to the Medes and Persians. That very night, Belshazzar died, and Darius the Mede became king.

Dan. 5:1–31

BENAIAH

Benaiah was a commander over thirty brave warriors who protected David when he fled from King Saul. After David took the throne, Benaiah was in charge of twenty-four thousand troops. Benaiah was always faithful to David and helped his son Solomon become king. Later, Benaiah

carried out Solomon's orders to kill three men who had
betrayed David.

2 Sam. 23:20–22; 1 Kings 1:38–40; 2:13–46; 1 Chron. 27:5–6

BENJAMIN

Benjamin was the twelfth and youngest son of Jacob. His
mother was Rachel. When a famine hit Canaan, Jacob sent
his sons to buy grain in Egypt. Fearing for Benjamin's life,
Jacob kept him at home. But Joseph demanded that his
brothers return with Benjamin, and Jacob agreed to let him
go. When Joseph saw Benjamin, his full brother whom he
deeply loved, he went to his room and wept.

Gen. 35:16–18; 42:1–4

BEZALEL

God chose Bezalel to be the chief designer of the
tabernacle's furnishings. God filled him with wisdom,
understanding, knowledge, and skill for his tasks. Bezalel's
assistant was Oholiab.

Ex. 31:1–6

BILHAH AND ZILPAH

Bilhah and Zilpah were maidservants to Jacob's two wives,
Rachel and Leah. Bilhah served Rachel, and Zilpah served
Leah. Whenever Rachel and Leah couldn't conceive
children, they gave their maidservants to Jacob (a common
custom at the time). Bilhah bore Dan and Naphtali, and
Zilpah bore Gad and Asher.

Gen. 30:1–12

BOAZ

Boaz lived in Bethlehem during the period of the judges in Israel. His mother was Rahab. Boaz married Ruth, a woman from Moab. They had a child who was an ancestor of King David and Jesus Christ.

Ruth 2:1–4:22; Matt 1:5–6, 16

CAESAR AUGUSTUS

Augustus was Rome's first official emperor. He held power at the time of Jesus's birth. Augustus ordered the census that caused Joseph and Mary to travel to Bethlehem, where Jesus was born.

Luke 2:1–7

CAIAPHAS

Caiaphas was the powerful Jewish high priest during the ministry of Christ and the early years of the church. He declared that if the Jewish people continued to believe Jesus was their king, the Romans would fear a rebellion and take away their temple. Caiaphas said that Jesus should die instead of putting the entire Jewish nation at risk.

John 11:45–53; 18:12–14; Acts 4:5–21

19

CAIN AND ABEL

Cain was Adam and Eve's first son, and Abel was their second. Cain became a farmer, and Abel a shepherd. When Abel presented an offering from his flock, God was pleased. But when Cain brought God an offering of his crops, God rejected it because his heart was faithless. Cain grew angry and jealous and spitefully killed his brother. God punished Cain by sending him far from home, forced to wander and face danger. Yet God was merciful and placed a mark on Cain that warned others not to kill him.

Gen. 4:1–16; Heb. 11:4

CALEB

Caleb was one of the twelve spies sent to explore the promised land of Canaan. When they returned, only Caleb and Joshua had faith that God would help them conquer the people there. The other Israelites were afraid and wanted to return to Egypt. God was angry and proclaimed that Israel would wander in the desert for forty years. Joshua and Caleb were the only ones who survived to enter the promised land. At age eighty-five, Caleb inherited land he had explored at age forty.

Num. 13:1–14:38; Josh. 14:1–14

CLAUDIUS

The Roman emperor Claudius commanded that Jewish people living in Rome had to leave. Priscilla and Aquila, Jewish Christians, were forced to go to Corinth. There they became friends and ministry partners with the apostle Paul.

It was also during Claudius's reign that a severe famine affected his empire. The famine prompted the Christians in Antioch to send an offering to the church in Jerusalem.

Acts 11:27–30; 18:1–4

CORNELIUS

Cornelius was a God-seeking Roman military officer. He received a vision from God instructing him to find the apostle Peter. Peter preached the gospel to Cornelius, and Cornelius and his household believed and were baptized. When Peter told this story to the Jewish Christians who lived in Jerusalem, they praised God for including gentiles in his plan of salvation.

Acts 10:1–11:18

CYRUS

This Persian king declared that the exiled Jewish people in his land should return to Jerusalem to rebuild the temple. More than a century earlier, Isaiah had prophesied that Cyrus would play a special role in helping God's people.

2 Chron. 36:15–23; Isa. 44:28–45:1, 13

DAN

Dan was the fifth son of Jacob. He was born to Rachel's maidservant, Bilhah, when Rachel was desperate to give Jacob children. The name Dan means "He has vindicated."

Gen. 30:1–6

DANIEL

Daniel was part of the first wave of Jewish nobles who were exiled to Babylon. There he was renamed Belteshazzar. Daniel was an intelligent young man and faithful to God. While training for service in the king's court, he chose not to eat the rich food he was served. Daniel did well in his studies and interpreted mysterious dreams and messages God gave to the kings he served. But Daniel got into serious trouble when he would not obey a decree to pray to King Darius. Daniel was thrown into a den of lions, but God saved Daniel by sending an angel. During his life, Daniel fasted and prayed for Jerusalem to be restored. He also had several powerful visions of end-times events.

Dan. 1:1–2:49; 4:1–5:31; 6:1–28; 9:1–12:13

DARIUS

Darius is often used as a title for Persian kings. The books of Ezra, Haggai, and Zechariah refer to Darius I, who supported the rebuilding of the temple. The Darius in the book of Nehemiah could be Darius II. And the reference in the book of Daniel is to Darius the Mede, the famous king who had Daniel thrown into the lions' den. When God saved Daniel, this King Darius proclaimed that everyone in his kingdom must worship the one true God.

Ezra 4:5, 24; 5:1–6:12; Neh. 12:22; Dan. 5:30–6:27

DAUGHTERS OF ZELOPHEHAD

As the Israelites approached the promised land, the five daughters of Zelophehad—Mahlah, Noah, Hoglah, Milkah, and Tirzah—courageously appeared before the whole assembly. Because their father died without a male heir, they requested their father's inheritance of land. Moses consulted God, who agreed with the daughters. They inherited property and preserved their father's name.

Num. 27:1–11; 36:1–12

DAVID, KING

David was a shepherd, warrior, fugitive, king, sinner, and writer of psalms. He was also an ancestor of Jesus, the Messiah. After King Saul disobeyed God, God chose David to be king. God was pleased with David because he was "a man after his own heart." David didn't take his throne until many years later, however, because he refused to take it from

Saul by force. In the meantime, David was a great warrior in Saul's army. He killed the giant Goliath and led the Israelites to win many battles. This made Saul jealous, and he tried to kill David. David spent years on the run trying to escape Saul. When Saul was finally killed in battle, David became king and brought together the tribes of Israel. Yet David was not immune to sin or suffering. He committed adultery and murder, and two of his sons died trying to take his throne. Throughout his life, however, David sought the Lord and confessed his wrongdoing. God loved David deeply and promised that one of his descendants would sit on the throne of Israel forever. God's promise was fulfilled through Jesus Christ, who descended from David.

1 Sam. 15:10–1 Kings 2:25; Matt. 1:1

DEBORAH AND BARAK

Deborah was a prophetess and judge in Israel. She called on Barak to battle the Canaanites, but he would not go without her. God was with them and gave Israel a great victory. Deborah continued her leadership of Israel with forty years of peace.

Judg. 4:1–5:31

DELILAH

Delilah was a Philistine woman who became the lover of Samson, a judge of Israel. Delilah was offered a bribe by the Philistines to discover the source of Samson's strength. She tried, but three times he deceived her. The fourth time, he gave in to Delilah's charms. After he told her the truth, Delilah betrayed Samson to his enemies.

Judg. 16:4–21

DINAH

Dinah was Jacob's only daughter. When their family moved to Canaan, Dinah was defiled by Shechem. Afterward, Shechem asked Dinah's brothers to allow him to marry her. They pretended to agree but took revenge instead. Two of Dinah's brothers killed every man in Shechem's city.

Gen. 34:1–31

ELEAZAR THE HIGH PRIEST

Eleazar was the third son of Aaron, Israel's first high priest. Eleazar was head of the Levites and responsible for the inside of the tabernacle. After Aaron passed away, Eleazar became the high priest and assisted Moses. When Moses died, Eleazar helped Joshua lead Israel into the promised land. He also helped assign Israel's tribal territories.

Num. 3:2–3, 32; 20:25–28; 26:1–3; 27:18–23; 34:16–17

ELI THE HIGH PRIEST

Eli was Israel's high priest during the period of the judges. Sadly, Eli honored his wicked sons more than he honored God. As a result, God declared he would judge Eli and his descendants. When Eli heard that his sons died in a battle, he fell off his chair, broke his neck, and died.

1 Sam. 1:1–4:18

ELIEZAR OF DAMASCUS

Eliezar was Abraham's chief servant. At Abraham's request, Eliezar made a long journey to find a wife for Abraham's son Isaac. Eliezar prayed for help with this task, and God directed him to Rebekah. She demonstrated a servant's heart by offering water to him and his camels. Eliezar gave Rebekah many expensive gifts and met with her family. The next day, Rebekah went with Eliezar to marry Isaac.

Gen. 15:2; 24:1–67

ELIJAH

Elijah was one of Israel's greatest prophets. God raised him up at a time when people in the northern kingdom had turned away from him to worship idols. Elijah performed amazing miracles and put the false prophets of Baal to shame on Mount Carmel. He warned King Ahab and Queen Jezebel that God would judge their wicked deeds. Although Ahab and Jezebel tried to kill Elijah, he escaped into the wilderness. God encouraged him there and gave him a new assignment. Later, God took Elijah to heaven in a most interesting way: He sent a chariot of fire to take Elijah up in a whirlwind.

1 Kings 17:1–19:18; 21:17–29; 2 Kings 1:1–2:12

ELISHA

The prophet Elisha was mentored by Elijah. After Elijah was taken to heaven, Elisha continued the work Elijah had started. In many ways, Elisha's ministry mirrored Elijah's. He raised the dead, challenged kings, and miraculously fed people for a long time with just a little food. God's power was so present in Elisha that even after Elisha died, a dead man came back to life when his body was thrown into Elisha's tomb.

1 Kings 19:16–21; 2 Kings 2:1–9:3; 13:14–21

ELIZABETH

After Elizabeth became pregnant in her old age, she was visited by her cousin Mary. At the sound of Mary's voice, Elizabeth's baby moved inside of her. Elizabeth was filled with the Holy Spirit and knew that Mary's baby was Israel's promised Messiah. Elizabeth's baby grew up to be John the Baptist, who prepared people's hearts to welcome Jesus Christ, the Messiah.

Luke 1:5–45; 57–80

ENOCH

Enoch was an ancestor of Noah and a humble man who walked faithfully with God. When he was 365 years old, God took him to heaven without dying.

Gen. 5:21–29

EPHRAIM AND MANASSEH

Ephraim and Manasseh were Joseph's sons. But their grandfather Jacob claimed them as his own sons. When Jacob was dying, he gave them a special blessing. Although Ephraim was younger, Jacob said that Ephraim would be greater than Manasseh. Jacob gave Ephraim the birthright (a double portion of inheritance) that usually belonged to the oldest son.

Gen. 41:50–52; 46:20; 48:1–20

ESAU

Esau and his brother, Jacob, were twins born to Isaac and Rebekah. Because Esau was born first, the birthright belonged to him. But Esau foolishly exchanged his birthright for stew that Jacob had made. Later, Jacob deceived Isaac into giving him the firstborn blessing meant for Esau. Esau planned to kill Jacob in revenge, but Jacob escaped. Twenty years later, after Esau was no longer angry, the brothers made peace. Esau's descendants were known as Edomites. They eventually became enemies of Jacob's descendants, the Israelites.

Gen. 25:19–34; 27:1–45; 33:1–17; 36:1–9; Ezek. 35:1–15

ESTHER, QUEEN

When Esther was born, she lived among the Jewish exiles in Persia. Because of her beauty and God's favor, King Xerxes chose her as his queen. Soon after, a powerful noble planned to destroy the Jewish people. Esther fasted for three days and urged her fellow Jews to do the same. Then she courageously appeared before the king and told him about the murderous plot. The king was outraged and allowed the Jews to defend themselves. The festival of Purim was established to celebrate this victory.

Esther 2:5–17; 4:7–17; 7:1–9:32

EUNICE AND LOIS

Timothy's mother Eunice and his grandmother Lois raised him to have a genuine faith in God. Timothy became Paul's disciple and eventually a pastor in Ephesus.

Acts 16:1–3; 2 Tim. 1:5

EVE

God created the first woman, Eve, from Adam's rib. God brought her to Adam, and as husband and wife they tended the garden of Eden. The serpent convinced her to disobey God by eating fruit from the Tree of Knowledge of Good and Evil. She offered it to Adam as well. God was grieved and punished Eve with painful childbearing. Yet God promised that one of her offspring would destroy the evil serpent. Eve gave birth to Cain, Abel, Seth, and likely other sons and daughters. God's promise to Eve was eventually fulfilled through Jesus Christ, who descended from Seth.

Gen. 2:15–3:16, 20; 4:1–2, 25; 5:4

EZEKIEL

Ezekiel was among the Jewish people who were captured and taken to Babylon. When he was thirty years old, God called him to be a prophet to his fellow exiles. Ezekiel's prophecies were a severe judgment against the rebellion of God's people. However, they also contained a hopeful and comforting reminder that God's good plans would still come to pass.

Ezek. 1:1; 2:1–10; 36:16–38

EZRA

Ezra was a Jewish priest and scholar who lived in Persia. With the help of King Artaxerxes, he led a second group of Jewish exiles back to Jerusalem. Ezra taught God's laws to the returning community. He wanted to ensure they would avoid the sins that had led Israel into exile.

Ezra 7:1–12; Neh. 8:2–6

FELIX

Felix was a Roman governor of Judea. He kept the apostle Paul locked up in prison for two years to gain favor with the Jewish people. Felix also hoped he would be bribed to release Paul.

Acts 23:23–24:27

FESTUS

Festus replaced Felix as governor of Judea. The chief priests and leaders in Jerusalem brought their case against the apostle Paul to him. When Festus asked Paul to go to Jerusalem and stand trial, Paul appealed to Caesar. Festus then listened as Paul shared his testimony of faith before King Agrippa II. Festus accused Paul of being insane.

Acts 24:27–26:32

GABRIEL

Gabriel is an angel who delivered important messages to God's people. He explained to the prophet Daniel the meaning of two of his visions. Much later, Gabriel announced to the priest Zechariah that his wife would have a baby in her old age. Soon after he visited Zechariah, Gabriel told Mary that she would give birth to Jesus, the Savior of mankind and promised Messiah of Israel.

Dan. 8:15–26; 9:20–27; Luke 1:11–20; 26–37

GAD

Gad was the seventh son of Jacob. His mother was Zilpah, Leah's maidservant. Leah gave Zilpah to Jacob because she had not become pregnant since giving birth to Judah.

Gen. 30:9–11

GAMALIEL

Gamaliel was a respected scholar and Pharisee who convinced the Jewish leaders not to execute the apostles. Gamaliel believed that if what they preached was false, Christianity would quickly die out on its own. If it was true, they would be disobeying God by not allowing their teaching. While defending himself before a violent crowd in Jerusalem, the apostle Paul revealed that he had studied under Gamaliel before becoming a Christian.

Acts 5:27–40; 22:3

GEDALIAH

When King Nebuchadnezzar of Babylon invaded Judah, he captured many of Judah's citizens but allowed some to stay. Nebuchadnezzar appointed Gedaliah to govern them. Gedaliah encouraged the people to farm the land and serve Nebuchadnezzar. Gedaliah was killed by one of his fellow Jews who betrayed him to the king of Ammon. After this, a group of Jews fled to Egypt because they did not feel safe.

2 Kings 25:1–25; Jer. 40:7–41:18

GEHAZI

Gehazi was Elisha's servant. When Elisha healed Naaman's leprosy, Gehazi was upset that Elisha refused Naaman's gifts. Naaman left, but Gehazi ran after him and lied to obtain the gifts. When Gehazi returned, he hid the gifts for himself. Elisha knew what Gehazi had done and announced that Gehazi and his descendants would have leprosy forever. Gehazi left the room and instantly became a leper.

2 Kings 4:12; 5:20–27

GENTILES

The word *gentiles* refers to people who are not Israelites. The prophets said the Messiah would restore Israel and also be "a light for the Gentiles." The New Testament teaches that gentiles are included in God's plan of salvation through Jesus Christ. The term *Greek* is sometimes used for *gentile*.

Ezra 6:21; Isa. 49:6; Acts 14:27; Gal. 3:8, 28–29

GIDEON

God allowed the nation of Midian to persecute Israel because the people had turned away from him. When the Israelites cried out to God for help, he raised up Gideon, Israel's fifth judge and a strong warrior. Gideon is famous for using a fleece to confirm God's call to leadership. He asked God to make the fleece wet with dew while the ground stayed dry, and then he asked for the fleece to stay dry while the ground became wet. God answered both requests. After Gideon gathered his army, God reduced the number of his troops from 32,000 to only 300. God did this so the Israelites would not think they defeated the Midianites on their own.

Judg. 6:1–16, 36–40; 7:1–25

GOLIATH

Goliath was a giant Philistine warrior who spoke disrespectfully about God and mocked the Israelite army. As a young man, David took up the challenge to slay Goliath. He did this even when older and stronger warriors were afraid of the giant. David killed Goliath wearing no armor and using only a slingshot. His heroic deed made him famous in Israel.

1 Sam. 17:4–54; 18:6–7

HABAKKUK

Habakkuk was a prophet who delivered God's message to Judah a short time before they fell to the Babylonians. Habakkuk couldn't understand why God would use a wicked nation like Babylon to bring justice to his own people. He struggled with how God's anger and justice related to his love and mercy. In the end, Habakkuk took comfort knowing that God would punish the wicked and redeem his people.

Hab. 1:12–2:1; 3:1–19

HAGAR

Hagar was Sarah's Egyptian servant. Sarah was barren, so she gave Hagar to Abraham. She hoped that Hagar would bear the son God had promised to Abraham. Hagar gave birth to Ishmael, but God had a different plan. He revealed to Abraham that despite Sarah's age, he had chosen her to bear the child he promised. Hagar and Sarah had a difficult relationship. Hagar and Ishmael eventually left and lived in the desert, where God cared for them.

Gen. 16:1–16; 21:1–21

HAGGAI

Haggai was a prophet to the Jewish people who had returned to Jerusalem from Babylon. God's message through Haggai pointed out that these Jews were residing in nice houses while his temple lay in ruins. Along with the prophet Zechariah, Haggai urged them to continue rebuilding the temple.

Ezra 5:1–2; 6:14; Hag. 1:1–15

HAMAN

Haman was the main adviser to King Xerxes of Persia. When a Jewish man named Mordecai refused to bow down to Haman, Haman planned to kill Mordecai. Haman also convinced the king to order that all Jews in his kingdom be destroyed. Queen Esther told the king about Haman's wicked plot and revealed that she, too, was Jewish. The king was furious at Haman and ordered him killed and the Jews saved.

Esther 3:1–4:17; 7:1–14

HANNAH

Hannah was Elkanah's favorite wife. Yet she remained childless while Elkanah's other wife continued to have children. Hannah prayed to God for a son, and he blessed her with a baby named Samuel. She devoted him to God's service in the tabernacle at Shiloh.

1 Sam. 1:1–28

HEROD AGRIPPA I

Called "King Herod" in Acts 12:1, he was the grandson of Herod the Great. Herod Agrippa I ruled during the early years of the church. He arrested members of the church in Jerusalem and executed the apostle James, the brother of John. Herod also arrested the apostle Peter, but an angel freed him from prison. When Herod gave a speech in Caesarea, the people were in awe and worshiped him as a god. Herod allowed them to do this and did not give praise to God, so an angel struck him dead.

Acts 12:1–23

HEROD AGRIPPA II

Also known as "King Agrippa," he was the son of Agrippa I. He and his sister Bernice listened closely to Paul's testimony when he was a prisoner in Caesarea. King

Agrippa declared that if Paul had not appealed to Caesar, he could have been freed.

Acts 25:13–26:32

HEROD ANTIPAS

Herod Antipas was a son of Herod the Great. Antipas ruled over Galilee, the location for much of Jesus's ministry. Antipas imprisoned and beheaded John the Baptist, who had condemned Antipas's wicked behavior. Antipas also wanted to kill Jesus. When Jesus learned this, he remarked that he was not afraid to continue healing people and casting out demons. Later, Antipas questioned and mocked Jesus at his trial.

Matt. 14:3–10; Luke 3:19; 13:31–33; 23:1–12

HEROD ARCHELAUS

Herod Archelaus was a son of Herod the Great. He ruled Judea after his father died. When Joseph heard this, he moved his family from Judea to Nazareth to protect Jesus.

Matt. 2:19–23

HEROD THE GREAT

Herod the Great was the ruler of Judea when Jesus was born. When Herod heard that wise men from the East came to Jerusalem looking for a newborn king, he became paranoid. To keep his position as king, Herod ordered the murder of all male children two years and under in Bethlehem. To protect Jesus, God gave Joseph a dream instructing him to take Jesus and Mary to Egypt.

Matt. 2:1–18

HERODIAS

Herodias divorced her husband to marry Herod Antipas. When John the Baptist spoke against this, Herodias became angry. Some time later, Herodias's daughter danced for Herod on his birthday. This pleased Herod so much that he promised her whatever she wanted. Herodias told her daughter to ask for the head of John the Baptist. Herod agreed and arranged for John's death.

Matt. 14:1–12

HEZEKIAH, KING

Hezekiah, Judah's thirteenth king, wisely led his kingdom during a period of threats from Assyria. He turned the people of Judah back to worshiping God. Counseled and encouraged by the prophet Isaiah, Hezekiah opened the temple's doors and celebrated Passover. He was unique among all the kings of Judah and stayed completely faithful to the Lord.

2 Kings 18:1–20:21;
2 Chron. 28:27–32:33;
Isa. 36:1–39:8

HIRAM

Hiram was the king of Tyre when David and Solomon were kings in Israel. Hiram was a good friend to both of them. He sent cedarwood and craftsmen to build David's palace. Later Hiram sent Solomon workmen, wood, and other costly materials to build the temple. In exchange, Solomon provided Hiram's household with food. Hiram also sent sailors to help guide Solomon's ships.

2 Sam. 5:11; 1 Kings 5:1–12; 9:14, 27

HOSEA

Hosea was a prophet to the Northern Kingdom of Israel. He served during a time of moral decline when Israel was turning to false gods. God instructed Hosea to marry an unfaithful woman, Gomer. His marriage served as a real-life example of Israel's unfaithfulness to God and God's unfailing love for his people.

Hos. 1:1–11

HOSHEA, KING

Hoshea was the last king of the northern tribes of Israel. When Hoshea failed to pay tribute to Assyria, Assyria's king attacked Samaria, imprisoned Hoshea, and removed the people from the land. They never returned.

2 Kings 15:30; 17:1–6

HULDAH

The prophetess Huldah told King Josiah that the kingdom of Judah would be judged for their sins. But because Josiah had humbled himself and sought the Lord, God would not send judgment in his lifetime. Four wicked kings ruled after Josiah, which led to Judah's eventual downfall.

2 Kings 22:14–20

HUR

Hur was an assistant to Moses and Aaron after the Israelites escaped from Egypt. When the Israelites fought the Amalekites, Hur helped hold up Moses's hands so the Israelites would be victorious. When Moses left the camp to meet with God on Mount Sinai, Hur helped resolve disputes among the people.

Ex. 17:8–13; 24:12–14

HUSHAI

Hushai was a loyal adviser to King David. When David's son Absalom rebelled, Hushai spied on Absalom by acting like he was on Absalom's side. Hushai offered Absalom counsel that would give David time to escape. Absalom accepted Hushai's advice, which led to David's victory.

2 Sam. 15:32–37; 16:15–17:23

ISAAC

Isaac was the son God promised to give Abraham and Sarah in their old age. His name means "laughter." When Isaac was growing up, God tested Abraham's faith by asking him to offer Isaac as a sacrifice. Right before Abraham was ready to kill Isaac, God provided a sacrificial ram instead. At age forty, Isaac married Rebekah. At age sixty, he became the father of twins Esau and Jacob. Isaac finished out his years living near Jacob's family in Hebron.

Gen. 21:1–7; 22:1–2, 13; 25:20, 26; 35:27–29

ISAIAH

Isaiah prophesied during the reign of four kings of Judah. It was during this time that Assyria conquered Israel and oppressed Judah. Isaiah delivered messages of judgment but also of hope in a coming Messiah.

2 Kings 19:1–20:19; 2 Chron. 26:22; 32:20; Isa. 3:1–26; 8:1–4; 53:1–12

ISHMAEL

Ishmael was born to Sarah's servant Hagar. Ishmael treated Isaac badly, so Hagar and Ishmael were sent away. Hagar arranged for Ishmael to marry an Egyptian, and Ishmael had many descendants. Throughout his life, Ishmael was hostile toward his relatives.

Gen. 16:1–16; 17:17–21; 21:8–21

ISSACHAR

Issachar was the ninth son of Jacob. His mother was Leah.
Issachar was conceived after Rachel made a bargain. She
traded with Leah, exchanging a night with Jacob for Leah's
son's mandrakes.

Gen. 30:14–18

JACOB (ISRAEL)

Jacob was Isaac's youngest son and a grandson of Abraham.
God chose Jacob to fulfill the promises he had made to
Abraham and Isaac. Jacob's name means "he deceives,"
and Jacob lived up to it. Jacob deceived his brother and his
father so he could have the blessing of the firstborn. Jacob
agreed to work seven years so he could marry his
uncle Laban's youngest daughter, Rachel. But
Laban tricked Jacob and gave him his oldest
daughter, Leah, instead. Jacob got to marry
Rachel, too, but in exchange for another
seven years of work. After working
for Laban twenty years, Jacob
returned to Canaan. On his
journey back, Jacob wrestled
with God. God renamed
Jacob *Israel*, which means "He
struggles with God." When Jacob
was old, he moved his family to Egypt
to escape a famine. Jacob's descendants
are known as the twelve tribes of Israel.

Gen. 25:19–34; 27:1–31:21; 32:22–32; 46:1–50:14

The Twelve Tribes of Israel	
1. Reuben	7. Gad
2. Simeon	8. Asher
3. Levi	9. Issachar
4. Judah	10. Zebulun
5. Dan	11. Joseph
6. Naphtali	12. Benjamin

JAEL

During a battle between Israel and Canaan, the commander of the Canaanite army (Sisera) fled to Jael's tent. He thought he would be safe there because she was not an Israelite. After Jael gave him something to drink, Sisera decided to take a nap. Jael then killed him with a tent peg while he slept. She became a hero to the Israelites.

Judg. 4:17–22

JAIRUS

This synagogue ruler in Capernaum begged Jesus to come and heal his desperately ill daughter. When the girl died before they arrived, Jesus encouraged Jairus to believe and then raised the girl from the dead.

Mark 5:22–24; 35–43

JAMES, BROTHER OF JESUS

James did not believe that Jesus was Israel's Messiah until after Jesus rose from the dead. Then James became the leader of the church in Jerusalem. At the Jerusalem Council, James supported Paul's case for accepting gentile believers as part of God's chosen people. He is also the author of the New Testament book of James.

Matt. 13:55; John 7:3–5; Acts 15:12–21; 1 Cor. 15:7; Gal. 2:9; James 1:1

JAMES, SON OF ALPHAEUS

He was one of the twelve disciples, but little else is known about him. He was also called "James the Younger" and "James the Less." Since the disciple Matthew is described in Mark 2:14 as "the son of Alphaeus," some believe that James and Matthew were brothers.

Matt. 10:3; Mark 2:14; 3:18; Luke 6:15

JAMES, SON OF ZEBEDEE

James was one of Jesus's twelve disciples. His brother, John, was also a disciple. Before this, both of them were in the fishing business with their father Zebedee. James and John were part of Jesus's inner circle. James became the first apostle to die for his faith, at the command of Herod Agrippa.

Matt. 4:21; Luke 9:28; Acts 12:1–2

JEHOSHAPHAT, KING

Jehoshaphat, the fourth king of Judah, continued the spiritual reforms of his father Asa. During his reign, the kingdoms of Judah and Israel were at peace. He even joined King Ahab of Israel in battle against Aram.

1 Kings 22:1–50; 2 Chron. 17:1–21:1

JEHOSHEBA

Jehosheba saved Joash, the next in line to Judah's throne, from being murdered by wicked Athaliah. By hiding him in the temple for six years, she was able to preserve the line of Judah's kings.

2 Chron. 22:10–12

JEHU, KING

Jehu was appointed by God to become the tenth king of the northern tribes of Israel. Elisha sent one of his prophets to anoint Jehu king and told him to destroy wicked king Ahab and his family. Jehu listened to Elisha and killed Ahab, his wife Jezebel, and all who had served Ahab or were related to him.

2 Kings 9:1–10:36; 2 Chron. 22:7–9

JEPHTHAH

Jephthah was a judge in Israel. When he was ready to lead his army against the Ammonites, he unwisely promised to sacrifice whatever came out of his house first if God helped him defeat the Ammonites. When Jephthah returned victorious, his daughter was the first to come out and greet him. Jephthah was devastated, and so was his daughter. She spent two months grieving that she would never marry and have children.

Judg. 11:29–40

JEREMIAH

The prophet Jeremiah warned that God would allow the Babylonians to invade Judah because the people had acted wickedly. Jeremiah's prophecies were direct and powerful, and he was strongly opposed by false prophets. Jeremiah was known as the "weeping prophet" because he often expressed to God the sorrow he felt from delivering such a difficult message. Yet Jeremiah also brought hope by proclaiming that God would make a new covenant with his people. After Babylon invaded Judah, a group of his fellow Jews took Jeremiah to Egypt against his will.

Jer. 1:1–19; 15:1–21; 28:1–17; 31:33–34; 43:4–7

JEROBOAM I, KING

Jeroboam led the northern tribes of Israel in rebellion against King Rehoboam of Judah. Jeroboam established the Northern Kingdom of Israel, but he also led them to worship idols. God struck him dead for his sins.

1 Kings 11:26–14:20; 2 Chron. 9:29–13:20

JEROBOAM II, KING

Jeroboam II was the thirteenth ruler of the Northern Kingdom of Israel. He fulfilled the words of Jonah the prophet and restored much of the land Israel had lost to Aram. Like the kings before him, he continued to worship false gods.

2 Kings 14:23–29

JESSE

Jesse was a shepherd from Bethlehem and the father of King David. The prophet Samuel came to Jesse with the news that God had selected one of his sons to become Israel's next king. Jesse presented seven of his sons before Samuel, but God did not choose them. To Jesse's surprise, God had chosen his youngest son, David. Throughout much of the Bible, David is referred to as "the son of Jesse." The prophet Isaiah declared that the Messiah of Israel would descend from Jesse.

1 Sam. 16:1–13; 1 Chron. 10:14; Isa. 11:10; Matt. 1:5–6; Acts 13:22

JETHRO

Jethro was a priest in Midian and the father-in-law of Moses. After Moses killed an Egyptian who was beating an Israelite, he fled to Midian. There he met Jethro's daughters and helped them water their flocks. Jethro was impressed and invited Moses to stay with him. Jethro also gave Moses his daughter Zipporah as a wife. When the Israelites were camped at Mount Sinai, Jethro came to visit Moses. He saw how hard Moses was working and advised him to appoint judges over small groups of people.

Ex. 2:11–21; 18:1–27

JEWS

The term *Jews* refer to the Jewish people, God's chosen people who descended from Jacob. The name comes from Jacob's fourth son, Judah, and the kingdom that was named after him. It was also known as Judea during the time of Jesus. The apostle Paul explained that God's plan of salvation through Jesus Christ began with the Jewish people. However, God intended for non-Jews (gentiles) to be included in this plan. Some Jews believed Jesus was God's promised Savior, and some didn't.

Ezra 5:1; Matt. 27:11; John 12:10–11; Gal. 2:28

JEZEBEL, QUEEN

Jezebel married Ahab, an evil king of the Northern Kingdom of Israel. She was a worshiper of the false god Baal. Arrogant and vengeful, Jezebel tried to kill the prophets of God. She especially went after Elijah because he had killed the prophets of Baal. Elijah prophesied that Jezebel would be thrown from a window and her body eaten by dogs. Her brutal death came to pass.

1 Kings 16:29–33; 19:1–2; 21:1–24; 2 Kings 9:1–37

JOAB

Joab was a nephew of King David and a longtime commander of his army. Joab was brave but could also be cruel. He killed King Saul's commander, who had killed his brother. Joab also killed David's rebellious son Absalom despite David's command not to harm him. After this, David removed Joab as commander. Joab proceeded to kill the new commander. Joab also sided with David's son Adonijah when he tried to claim David's throne. When David's son Solomon became king, he put Joab to death.

2 Sam. 3:26–27; 8:16; 11:1–24; 18:1–20:13;
1 Kings 1:5–2:35; 1 Chron. 2:13–16

JOB

Job was a righteous man who stayed away from evil. God allowed Satan to test Job's faith by taking away his children, livestock, servants, and health. Job's friends grieved with him and offered advice that wasn't always helpful. They questioned Job's innocence, but Job defended himself. He wondered why God had allowed him to suffer. God raised questions of his own with Job. As a result, Job focused on God's power and majesty instead of his suffering. He confessed his own limitations and saw God in a new light.

Job 1:6–2:13; 4:7; 13:1–19; 42:1–7

JOCHEBED

Jochebed was the mother of Aaron, Moses, and Miriam.
When Moses was born, she carefully hid him because
Pharaoh had ordered that all male Israelite babies must
be killed. After three months, Jochebed placed Moses in a
basket in the reeds of the Nile River. Pharaoh's daughter
found Moses and hired Jochebed to nurse him.

Ex. 1:22–2:10; Num. 26:59

JOEL

The prophet Joel called the people of Judah to turn from
their sins. Joel also spoke about the "day of the LORD,"
when God will pour out his Spirit on all nations. On
that day, he will judge his enemies and bring
salvation to his people.

Joel 1:15; 2:12, 28; 3:1–2, 20–21; Acts 2:16–21

JOHN, SON OF ZEBEDEE

John was one of Jesus's first
disciples. He and his brother
James were fishermen
before they became part of
Jesus's inner circle. Jesus referred
to them as "sons of thunder,"
probably because they wanted to
call down fire from heaven on a village
of Samaritans. John became one of Jesus's
closest friends and referred to himself as "the

disciple whom Jesus loved." John wrote the fourth gospel and the three New Testament letters that bear his name. While he was a prisoner on the island of Patmos, he wrote the book of Revelation. Tradition says John was the only apostle who was not killed because of their faith in Christ.

Matt. 4:18–22; Mark 3:17; Luke 9:52–56; John 13:23; Rev. 1:1

JOHN THE BAPTIST

John the Baptist was a bold prophet who lived in the wilderness near Jerusalem. He prepared the people of Judah to turn from their sins and follow Jesus. When large crowds came to hear John preach, he baptized those who wanted a right relationship with God. John proclaimed that Jesus was God's Son who would baptize God's people with the Holy Spirit. John was later executed for speaking out against the unlawful marriage of Herod Antipas.

Matt. 3:1–17; 14:1–11; John 1:29–36

JONAH

Jonah was a prophet who was supposed to deliver God's call of repentance to the city of Nineveh. Instead, he boarded a ship to Tarshish. When God sent a wind that stirred up a storm, the people on the ship threw Jonah overboard to save their lives. God sent a fish to swallow Jonah and keep him safe. Jonah cried out to God, and the fish spit Jonah up onshore. Jonah wasted no time and went to Nineveh to deliver God's message. The people of Nineveh turned from their sins, so God did not send judgment.

Jonah 1:1–3:10

JONATHAN

Jonathan was King Saul's oldest son and one of David's closest friends. Although Saul wanted to kill David, Jonathan and David made a promise they would always stay friends. David also promised to show kindness to Jonathan's family. Jonathan kept his promise by helping David escape from Saul. After Jonathan was killed in battle, David took care of Jonathan's son.

1 Sam. 13:16; 20:12–17; 31:1–2 Sam. 1:27

JOSEPH, MARY'S HUSBAND

Joseph was an honorable, quiet man and the husband of Mary, the mother of Jesus. God sent angels to deliver important instructions to Joseph, and Joseph obeyed. He acted like a father to Jesus, teaching him how to be a carpenter. Some believe Joseph may have died before Jesus began his public ministry.

Matt. 1:18–25; 2:13–23

JOSEPH OF ARIMATHEA

Joseph of Arimathea was a wealthy member of the Sanhedrin (the Jewish religious council) and a secret disciple of Jesus. He spoke against the Sanhedrin's plot to have Jesus arrested and sentenced to death. After Jesus died, Joseph helped prepare him for burial. Then he placed Jesus's body in a tomb that he owned.

Matt. 27:57–60; Luke 23:50–54; John 19:38–42

JOSEPH, SON OF JACOB

Joseph was Jacob's eleventh son, the first child that Rachel bore, and Jacob's favorite son. Jacob gave Joseph a special robe to wear, and this made Joseph's brothers jealous. They despised him even more when Joseph dreamed his family would bow down to him. Joseph's brothers hated him so much that they sold him into slavery. He ended up in Egypt. There he was falsely accused and put in prison, but God was with him. When Joseph explained the meaning of Pharaoh's dreams, he was released and made second in command. Joseph married an Egyptian and had two sons. Joseph was in charge of helping Egypt prepare for a famine. When his brothers came to buy grain, they had a tearful reunion. At Joseph's urging, Jacob and his family moved to Egypt. They enjoyed many years together before Joseph died.

Gen. 30:22–24; 37:1–36; 39:1–50:26

JOSHUA, SON OF NUN

Joshua was Moses's assistant and commander of the Israelite army. After the Israelites escaped from Egypt, Joshua led them in a victorious battle against the Amalekites. Later Joshua accompanied Moses on a journey up Mount Sinai so Moses could meet with God. After Moses died, Joshua led Israel into Canaan. He courageously led the Israelite army and helped defeat Israel's enemies in the promised land. Throughout his life, Joshua was faithful to God.

Ex. 17:9–13; 24:13; Num. 13:1–14:38; Josh. 1:1–9; 24:11–13

JOSHUA THE HIGH PRIEST

Joshua the High Priest traveled to Jerusalem with the first wave of returning Jewish exiles. With Zerubbabel, Joshua helped lead the rebuilding of the temple. The prophet Zechariah declared that Joshua was a symbol of the coming Messiah.

Ezra 2:1–2; 3:2; Zech. 3:8

JOSIAH, KING

Josiah became the sixteenth king of Judah at age eight. During his long reign, he brought about many spiritual reforms. The book of the law was found after a long absence, and the temple restored. Judah's covenant with God was renewed and Passover celebrated. Josiah died after he was wounded in a battle against Egypt.

2 Kings 21:26–23:30; 2 Chron. 33:25–35:27

JUDAH

Judah was the fourth son of Jacob. His mother was Leah. God chose one of Judah's descendants to bring Jesus Christ into the world, who would save his people from sin and death.

Gen. 29:31, 35; Matt. 1:1–3, 21

JUDAS ISCARIOT

Judas Iscariot was the disciple who stole money that others had generously donated to Jesus's ministry. Later he accepted thirty pieces of silver to turn Jesus over to the chief priests. After he betrayed Jesus, Judas was filled with remorse. He returned the money and hung himself.

Matt. 26:14–15; 27:3–5; John 6:70–71

JUDE

Jude wrote the book of the Bible bearing his name. In it he identified himself as "a brother of James." He was likely referring to the James who was well known as the Lord's brother and the leader of the Jerusalem church. This would also make Jude a brother of Jesus. He is called "Judas" (the Greek version of his name) in Matthew 13:55 and Mark 6:3.

Matt. 13:55; Mark 6:3; Gal. 2:8–9; Jude 1:1

KORAH

Korah led a rebellion when the Israelites were wandering in the desert. He was jealous that God had chosen Moses and Aaron to lead them. Because of the rebellion, God caused the ground to open and swallow up Korah, his family, and his followers.

Num. 16:1–34

LABAN

Laban was Rebekah's brother, Jacob's uncle, and the father of Leah and Rachel. Jacob worked for Laban as a shepherd for twenty years. During that time, Laban deceived and mistreated Jacob in many ways. God told Jacob to go back to Canaan, so Jacob and his family left in secret. Laban was angry when he found out, so he quickly pursued them. When Laban caught up with Jacob, they agreed to part ways but treat each other with respect in the future.

Gen. 24:29; 29:14–30; 31:1–55

LAZARUS, BROTHER OF MARY AND MARTHA

Lazarus and his sisters Mary and Martha of Bethany were good friends of Jesus. Four days after dying from an unknown illness, Jesus called Lazarus out of his tomb and restored him to life. Many Jews believed in Jesus because of this miracle.

John 11:1–44; 12:1–11

LEAH

Leah was Jacob's first wife. Because Jacob loved Rachel more than Leah, God showed her favor by giving her more children. Jesus Christ is a descendant of Leah's son Judah.

Gen. 29:21–30; 30:9–21; Matt. 1:1–3

LEVI

Levi was Jacob's third son. His mother was Leah. God set apart Levi's descendants to be priests and attendants in the tabernacle and temple. The Levites did not receive an inheritance of land, but God reserved cities just for them throughout Israel.

Gen. 29:34; Deut. 18:1–2; Num. 8:19; 35:1–3

LOT

Lot was Abraham's nephew. He went with Abraham and Sarah on their journey to Canaan. When it became clear that the land could not support them both, Abraham gave Lot his first choice of locations. Lot chose the area around Sodom, while Abraham settled in Canaan. When war broke out, Abraham rescued Lot and his family. Lot needed rescuing again when God was ready to destroy the wicked city of Sodom. Two angels led Lot and his family out of town. As they were fleeing, Lot's wife looked back and became a pillar of salt. After this, Lot and his daughters lived in the mountains with no hope for continuing their family line, so Lot's daughters slept with their father and became pregnant. Their descendants, the Moabites and

Ammonites, became enemies of the Israelites.

Gen. 11:27; 12:4–5; 13:1–13; 14:1–16; 19:1–38; Judg. 3:28; 11:36

LUKE

Luke was a gentile doctor who became a
ministry partner of the apostle Paul.
He is not named in the Gospels, but
Luke is credited with writing the
gospel that bears his name. He
is also credited with writing
its sequel, the book of Acts.

Luke 1:1–4; Acts 1:1–2; Phil. 1:24;
Col. 4:14; 2 Tim. 4:11

LYDIA

Lydia, a businesswoman and a gentile who
believed in God, became a Christian when
she heard Paul preach the gospel near Philippi.
Her entire household was baptized. Later Lydia welcomed
Paul and Silas into her home after they were released from
prison.

Acts 16:11–15, 40

MALACHI

The prophet Malachi called for spiritual renewal among
the people of Judah. It had been decades since they had
returned from exile and rebuilt the temple, yet the blessings
promised by previous prophets had not fully come to pass.
The Jewish people had largely given up on God. Malachi

reminded them that surely the day of God's justice would come. The wicked would face judgment, and the hearts of God's people would be renewed.

Mal. 1:1–9; 3:1–4; 4:5–6

MANASSEH, KING

Hezekiah's son Manasseh, who was made king at age twelve, led Judah astray for more than five decades. He worshiped Assyrian gods and killed many innocent people. Late in his life, he repented of his evil ways.

2 Kings 21:1–18; 2 Chron. 32:33–33:20

MARK (JOHN MARK)

Mark is not mentioned by name in the gospel of Mark, but he is considered its author. Some believe he may be the unnamed young man mentioned in Mark 14:51–52. Mark lived with his mother in Jerusalem and was a cousin of Barnabas. He went with the apostle Paul on his first missionary journey but left mid-trip. This caused a rift between Paul and Barnabas. Paul hesitated to take Mark on another trip, but Barnabas gave him a second chance. Mark eventually regained Paul's trust. He was also a friend of the apostle Peter.

Mark 14:51–52; Acts 12:12; 15:36–41;
Col. 4:10; 2 Tim. 4:11

MARY AND MARTHA

Sisters Mary and Martha of Bethany were close friends and followers of Jesus. While Mary listened to Jesus teach at their home, Martha kept busy with hosting. Martha asked Jesus to persuade Mary to help her. In reply, Jesus reminded Martha that Mary had chosen what was most important—sitting at his feet to listen and learn. The sisters' faith grew even stronger after they witnessed Jesus raise their brother Lazarus from the dead. Jesus said that Mary will always be remembered for anointing his feet with perfume shortly before he was crucified.

Luke 10:38–42; John 11:1–45; 12:1–11

MARY MAGDALENE

Mary Magdalene was possessed by seven evil spirits before Jesus cast them out. After that, Mary became one of Jesus's most devoted followers and supporters. She was present at Jesus's crucifixion and burial. Mary Magdalene encountered the risen Lord near his empty tomb and told the disciples what he said to her.

Matt. 27:57–61; Mark 15:25, 40; Luke 8:1–3; 23:49–24:11; John 20:1–18

MARY, MOTHER OF JESUS

When Mary was a young virgin, she was visited by an angel. He gave her surprising news: God favored her highly and had chosen her to give birth to his Son. She was to name him Jesus. Mary treasured this message in her heart. Years later, Mary called on Jesus when there was no more wine at a wedding. In response, he performed his first miracle by turning jugs of water into wine. Mary was with Jesus when he died on the cross. After Jesus ascended to heaven, Mary continued to pray with the believers. She was likely present with the other believers at Pentecost.

Luke 1:26–56; 2:4–5; John 2:1–12; 19:25–27; Acts 1:14

MATTHEW (LEVI)

Matthew, also called Levi, was a tax collector in Capernaum. He left his job to become a disciple of Jesus. He eventually wrote the gospel of Matthew, where he refers to himself as "Matthew the tax collector." Tax collectors had a reputation for being dishonest and greedy. Since the other Gospels do not state that he was a tax collector, Matthew may have wanted to highlight Jesus's gracious acceptance of sinners like himself.

Matt. 9:9; 10:3; Mark 2:13–15

MATTHIAS

Matthias and another man
were nominated to take
Judas Iscariot's place as one
of the twelve apostles. The
apostles prayed for guidance
and then cast lots. Matthias
was chosen. According to Greek
tradition, Matthias ministered in
Cappadocia, in modern-day Turkey. Some historians write
that he was eventually killed because of his faith.

Acts 1:15–26

MELCHIZEDEK

After Abraham rescued Lot from foreign invaders,
Melchizedek brought bread and wine to celebrate. The
Bible identifies Melchizedek as the king of Salem and
the priest of God Most High. His name means "king
of righteousness." Melchizedek prayed a blessing over
Abraham, and Abraham gave Melchizedek a tenth of his
spoils. The book of Hebrews points out that the priesthood
of Jesus Christ is like that of Melchizedek.

Gen. 14:1–20; Heb. 5:1–10; 6:19–7:28

MEPHIBOSHETH

Mephibosheth was Jonathan's son. When Saul and Jonathan
were killed, Mephibosheth's nurse picked him up to flee. In
her haste, she dropped Mephibosheth. His feet were hurt,

and he was permanently disabled. When David became king, he kept his promise to show kindness to Jonathan's family and took care of Mephibosheth. He was allowed to eat at the king's table for the rest of his life.

1 Sam. 20:14–17; 2 Sam. 4:4; 9:1–13; 21:7

METHUSELAH

Methuselah was the son of Enoch and an ancestor of Noah. Methuselah died at the age of 969, which is the longest life span recorded in the Bible.

Gen. 5:21–27

MICAH

Micah prophesied against the leaders of Israel and Judah for their injustice, greed, and lack of humility. Micah warned them of God's justice, the destruction of Samaria, and the fall of Jerusalem. Micah also proclaimed a vision of redemption and forgiveness. He promised that some of God's people would return from exile, regain their inheritance, and worship the Lord. He called God's people to justice, love, mercy, and humility.

Jer. 26:18; Mic. 1:1–16; 4:1–13; 6:8

MICHAEL THE ARCHANGEL

Michael is a powerful angel. When the Israelites were exiled to Persia, his role was to support and defend them. He helped the angel Gabriel when he was opposed by evil spiritual forces. The book of Revelation states that Michael will also help God's people during a time of distress in the end times.

Dan. 10:13, 21; 12:1; Jude 1:9; Rev. 12:7–9

MICHAL

Michal was King Saul's daughter. Saul gave her in marriage to David in return for an unusual dowry. Michal helped David escape when Saul went mad and tried to kill him. Saul eventually took Michal from David and gave her as a wife to another man. She was forcefully restored to David when he became king. Later Michal despised and mocked David for dancing joyfully in public. Michal died without having any children.

1 Sam. 18:17–30; 19:14–18; 6:16–23

MIRIAM

Miriam was a prophet and the sister of Moses and Aaron. She was likely the sister who helped Pharaoh's daughter rescue baby Moses from the Nile River. Miriam later led the Israelite women to sing and dance after they escaped Pharaoh's army. In the wilderness, however, she opposed Moses. God punished her with leprosy but soon restored her. Like the rest of her generation, she died before reaching the promised land.

Ex. 2:1–10; 15:19–21;
Num. 12:1–15; 20:1

MORDECAI

Mordecai was a Jewish man who lived in Persia during the time of Judah's exile. Mordecai was faithful to God and refused to bow to the king's adviser. In revenge, the adviser schemed to kill all the Jewish people in Persia. Mordecai found out his plans and urged his cousin, Queen Esther, to appeal to the king. When the king learned that Mordecai had uncovered a plot to kill him, the king made Mordecai second in command.

Est. 2:5–10:3

MOSES

Moses is perhaps the most important person in the Old Testament. He was a shepherd for forty years until God appeared to him in a burning bush. At God's direction, Moses led the Israelites out of slavery in Egypt. He then led them through the wilderness toward the promised land of Canaan. Moses represented Israel to God and God to Israel. He received the law from God on Mount Sinai and taught it to the Israelites. He is known as the author of the Torah, the first five books of the Bible. God did not allow Moses to enter the promised land, but he gave Moses a view of the land before he died.

Ex. 2:1–3:20; 14:1–31; 19:1–24:18;
Deut. 34:1–4; Luke 24:27

NAAMAN

Naaman was the army commander of Aram. When Naaman had leprosy, he went to the prophet Elisha's house to find healing. Elisha's messenger told Naaman to wash seven times in the nearby Jordan River. At first Naaman went away angry, expecting something more dramatic. But Naaman's servants convinced him to try it, and he was healed. Naaman pledged he would only worship the one true God—the God of Israel.

2 Kings 5:1–27; Luke 4:27

NAHUM

Nahum prophesied about God's plans to destroy the Assyrian capital of Nineveh. Assyria had captured and tortured the people in the Northern Kingdom of Israel. The Southern Kingdom of Judah also endured a century of cruel treatment from Assyria. God's word through Nahum was fulfilled when Nineveh fell to the Babylonians and Medes.

Nah. 1:12–15

NAOMI

During a famine in Judah, Naomi fled with her husband and sons to Moab. After they died, she learned the famine had ended. Naomi returned to Bethlehem with her daughter-in-law Ruth.

Naomi helped Ruth marry a relative of Naomi's who would care for them both.

Ruth 1:1–22; 4:13–22

NAPHTALI

Naphtali was the sixth son of Jacob. His mother was Bilhah, Rachel's servant. His name means "my struggle" and reflects Rachel's childbearing competition with Leah.

Gen. 30:7–8

NATHAN

Nathan was a prophet who advised King David. When David wanted to build a temple for God, Nathan prophesied that one of David's sons would carry out the task instead. This was fulfilled through King Solomon and ultimately Jesus Christ, who was a descendant of David and Solomon. When David committed adultery with Bathsheba, Nathan came to David with a clever parable that revealed David's sin. Nathan was also Solomon's record-keeper.

2 Sam. 7:1–17; 12:1–14; 2 Chron. 9:29

NEBUCHADNEZZAR

King Nebuchadnezzar of Babylon conquered Judah and destroyed the temple in Jerusalem. He ordered that leaders of Judah be killed, captured, or taken to Babylon. Because Nebuchadnezzar was proud and cruel, God caused him to live like a wild animal. After this experience,

Nebuchadnezzar changed his ways and gave God the honor he deserved.

2 Chron. 36:11–21; Jer. 25:1–14; Dan. 1–7; 2:1–48; 4:1–37

NEHEMIAH

Nehemiah was the cupbearer for the Persian king Artaxerxes. With the king's permission, Nehemiah led the third wave of Jewish exiles back to Jerusalem. He then served as governor of Judah and led the rebuilding of the walls of the city. Nehemiah faced fierce opposition from foreign neighbors. But under his strong leadership, the wall was eventually finished.

Neh. 1:1–2:20; 5:14; 6:1–15

NICODEMUS

A well-known member of the Jewish council (Sanhedrin), Nicodemus is mentioned only in the gospel of John. Nicodemus is best known for meeting with Jesus under the cover of night. Jesus told him that no one can enter God's kingdom unless they are born again. When Jewish leaders were condemning Jesus, Nicodemus defended him. Following Jesus's death, Nicodemus helped his fellow council member Joseph of Arimathea prepare Jesus for burial.

John 3:1–21; 7:50–52; 19:39–42

NOAH

During a time of terrible wickedness,
God decided to send a devastating
flood to the earth. But God
wanted to save Noah because
he was righteous. God
gave Noah detailed
instructions about how
to build a huge boat. When
the flood came, Noah and
his family and a pair of every
animal remained safe on the boat.
The land dried out, and Noah offered
sacrifices to thank God for his protection.
God responded by promising to never again
destroy the earth with a flood. He symbolized this
promise with the rainbow.

Gen. 5:28–10:17

OBADIAH

Obadiah delivered a short but strong message of judgment
against the nation of Edom. He announced that God would
punish them and other nations who had mistreated his
people in the neighboring kingdom of Judah. Obadiah also
prophesied that the exiles from Israel and Judah would
return to their land. He proclaimed that God himself
would be their king.

Obad. 1:1–2, 10, 15–17, 21

OMRI, KING

Omri, army commander of the Northern Kingdom of Israel, fought against Tibni to become Israel's sixth king. Omni was victorious and moved the capital of Israel from Tirzah to Samaria. He continued the practice of idol worship, which King Jeroboam had begun decades earlier.

1 Kings 16:15–28

PAUL (SAUL OF TARSUS)

Paul was first known by his Jewish name, Saul of Tarsus. He was a Pharisee who persecuted Christians before he had a miraculous encounter with Jesus. Saul believed and was baptized. After Paul proved his sincere faith to the Christians in Jerusalem, he traveled throughout the Roman empire preaching the gospel. He went on three missionary journeys and was imprisoned several times because of his faith. He performed countless miracles, healing people's illnesses and bringing the dead back to life. Paul was arrested again in Jerusalem and brought to Rome to stand trial before the emperor Nero. Tradition says that Paul was beheaded by Nero because of his faith in Christ. Paul wrote at least thirteen books in the New Testament.

Acts 7:58; 8:1–3; 9:1–30; 11:1–28:31

PETER

The apostle Peter was originally named Simon. Because he was bold in his belief that Jesus was the Messiah, Jesus gave him the nickname Cephas. This Aramaic word means "the rock." He was more commonly known by the name Peter, the Greek word for rock. This simple, impulsive man was a fisherman before Jesus called him to leave everything and follow him. Peter, James, and John formed Jesus's inner circle. During Jesus's trial, however, "the rock" crumbled under pressure. He denied that he even knew Jesus. Yet the resurrected Jesus forgave and restored Peter. Peter became a leader of the early church and wrote the books of 1 and 2 Peter. Tradition says he was crucified upside down because he didn't consider himself worthy to die the same way that Jesus did.

Matt. 4:18; 16:16; Luke 22:54–62; John 1:42; 21:1–17; 1 & 2 Peter 1:1

The Twelve Disciples	
1. Simon Peter	7. Thomas
2. Andrew	8. Matthew
3. James, Son of Zebedee	9. James, Son of Alphaeus
4. John	10. Thaddaeus
5. Philip	11. Simon the Zealot
6. Bartholomew (Nathanael)	12. Judas Iscariot (replaced by Matthias)

PHARAOH

Pharaoh is the title used for ancient kings of Egypt. Joseph became second in command of Egypt when he interpreted the pharaoh's dreams. Generations later, the pharaoh was a harsh and cruel slave master to the Israelites. God sent Moses to ask Pharaoh to release the Israelites. Pharaoh refused, so God struck Egypt with dreadful plagues.

Rameses II

When the Israelites escaped through the Red Sea, Pharaoh and his army drowned. Throughout most of Israel's history, Egypt's pharaoh made trouble for the Israelites. The prophets warned that God would judge him.

Gen. 41:1–40; Ex. 1:8–14:31; 2 Kings 23:29; Jer. 46:25; Ezek. 29:1

PHARISEES

The Pharisees were a powerful group of Jewish religious teachers during the time of Christ. They came up with their own laws and pushed the people to follow them. When Jesus challenged them for placing their teachings above the law of Moses, they became angry. They were also jealous of the miracles Jesus did and the number of followers he had.

Matt. 16:1–12; 23:1–36; Luke 6:1–11

PHILEMON

Philemon was a coworker of the apostle Paul. He hosted a church in his own home. Philemon also had a slave named

Onesimus. Onesimus decided to flee from Philemon and somehow met Paul. They became friends when Paul shared the gospel and Onesimus believed. Paul wrote a letter to Philemon asking him to take Onesimus back. Paul encouraged Philemon to treat Onesimus as a brother instead of a slave.

Philem. 1:1–20

PHILIP THE APOSTLE

Jesus called Philip to be one of his twelve disciples. Philip also invited his friend Nathanael to follow Jesus. When five thousand people flocked to Jesus, Philip decided that a half year's wages would not have bought food for everyone. According to tradition, Philip died for his faith in modern-day Turkey.

John 1:43–48; 6:1–7; 12:20–22

PHILIP THE EVANGELIST

This Philip was appointed with six other men to care for widows in the early church. He also preached and performed miracles in Samaria. Later he was instructed by an angel to meet an Ethiopian official. Philip obeyed and shared the gospel with him. After Philip baptized him, the Holy Spirit carried Philip away to a different place. He

preached the gospel as he made his way to Caesarea. Philip was referred to as "the evangelist" when the apostle Paul stayed with him in Caesarea. Philip had four daughters who prophesied.

Acts 6:1–6; 8:4–8, 26–40; 21:8–9

PHINEHAS, SON OF ELEAZAR

Phinehas was the son of Israel's second high priest, Eleazar, and a grandson of Aaron. When the Israelite men slept with Moabite women, Phinehas took action. He killed one of the men and his Moabite mistress. Because Phinehas brought justice, God promised that his descendants would be priests of Israel forever.

Ex. 6:25; Num. 25:1–13

PHOEBE

Phoebe was a deacon of the church in Cenchreae (in modern Greece). It's likely that she delivered Paul's letter to the Christians in Rome. Phoebe evidently was wealthy and used her money to support Paul and other Christians.

Rom. 16:1–2

PONTIUS PILATE

Pilate was the Roman governor during the ministry of Jesus. He is most famous for overseeing Jesus's trial. Pilate gave in to the crowd and released the criminal Barabbas instead of Jesus. He sentenced Jesus to die on the cross and sent guards to protect Jesus's tomb.

Matt. 27:1–2, 11–65

POTIPHAR

Potiphar was the captain of Pharaoh's guard. He bought Joseph as a slave after Joseph's brothers sold him to slave traders. Potiphar put Joseph in charge of his household, and God blessed Potiphar's affairs because of Joseph. When Potiphar's wife tried to seduce Joseph, Joseph refused to sin. She took revenge by falsely accusing Joseph of trying to sleep with her. Potiphar believed his wife and sent Joseph to prison.

Gen. 37:26–36; 39:1–20

QUEEN OF SHEBA

The queen of Sheba traveled to Jerusalem to meet King Solomon. She wanted to judge for herself the truth of King Solomon's wisdom, wealth, and power. She was from southern Arabia and gave Solomon gifts of gold, spices, and precious stones. After meeting with Solomon, she agreed that his fame was well deserved. She also recognized that Solomon had a close relationship with God. The queen returned home with many gifts from Solomon.

1 Kings 10:1–13; 2 Chron. 9:8

RACHEL

Rachel was the beloved second wife of Jacob. Jacob wanted to marry only her, but he was tricked into marrying Leah first. Rachel gave Jacob two sons: Joseph and Benjamin. Rachel died giving birth to Benjamin.

Gen. 29:9–30; 30:22–24; 35:16–26

RAHAB

Rahab was a Canaanite prostitute who lived in Jericho. She put her faith in God when she heard about the wonderful deeds God had done for Israel. Two Israelite men came to spy out the promised land, and Rahab hid them in her house. These men saved Rahab and her family when the Israelites attacked Jericho. Rahab married an Israelite, and they had a son named Boaz. Boaz was an ancestor of King David and Jesus Christ.

Josh. 2:1–21; 6:15–25; Matt. 1:1, 5

REBEKAH

When Abraham sent his servant to find a wife for Isaac, God made it clear he had chosen Rebekah. Rebekah willingly went with the servant and became Isaac's wife. She waited many years before God gave her children. When her twins wrestled in her womb, God showed Rebekah they would become separate nations. Rebekah gave birth to Esau first and Jacob second. Because Rebekah favored Jacob, she helped him deceive Isaac into giving Jacob the firstborn blessing.

Gen. 24:1–67; 25:19–34; 27:1–46

REHOBOAM, KING

After Solomon died, his son Rehoboam became Israel's next king. Rehoboam listened to foolish advisers and increased the heavy burdens Solomon had put on the northern tribes, so they rebelled and went to war against Rehoboam. The nation split into two kingdoms. Israel (northern tribes) was led by Jeroboam, and Judah (southern tribes) was led by Rehoboam. Sadly, Rehoboam led Judah to worship false gods and break God's laws.

1 Kings 11:43–12:24; 14:21–31; 2 Chron. 9:31–12:16

REUBEN

Reuben was the firstborn son of Jacob and his wife Leah. Reuben tried to rescue his younger brother Joseph when his jealous brothers wanted to kill him. He also slept with Jacob's concubine Bilhah. When Jacob was on his deathbed, he took away Reuben's birthright as the oldest son.

Gen. 29:31–32; 35:22; 37:18–30; 42:22; 49:3–4

RUTH

Ruth was a woman from Moab who displayed selfless devotion. She followed her mother-in-law, Naomi, to Naomi's home in Bethlehem. Ruth proclaimed that she would worship the God of Israel, as Naomi did. To provide for them both, Ruth gathered wheat in the field of Naomi's relative Boaz. Boaz was impressed by Ruth's hard work and love for Naomi. Boaz agreed to marry Ruth, and they had a son named Obed. Obed was an ancestor of King David and Jesus Christ.

Ruth 1:1–4:22; Matt. 1:5

SADDUCEES

The members of this Jewish religious group were priests. They dominated the Jewish ruling council (the Sanhedrin) during the time of Christ. The Sadducees often clashed with the Pharisees over their different beliefs, but they were united in opposing Jesus.

Matt. 3:7; 16:1–12; Luke 20:27–38

SAMARITAN WOMAN AT THE WELL

The Samaritan woman was drawing water from a well when Jesus, a Jew, asked her for a drink. Many Jews despised Samaritans, but Jesus had a long conversation with her. He told her everything she had done and explained that he was the Messiah promised in the Scriptures. When the woman told the townspeople what Jesus had said, they believed he was the Savior.

John 4:4–30, 39–42

SAMSON

Samson was an Israelite judge. Dedicated to the Lord as an infant,

Samson was destined to save Israel from the cruel Philistines. As part of his dedication, Samson was not allowed to cut his hair, which was the key to his great strength. But Samson's Philistine lover, Delilah, tricked him into sharing his secret. When Samson was asleep, Delilah had someone cut his hair. Samson's strength left him, and the Philistines captured him. But Samson asked God to strengthen him once more, then pushed against the pillars of the Philistine temple. It crumbled to the ground, killing many Philistines and Samson himself.

Judg. 13:1–16:31

SAMUEL

Samuel was dedicated to the Lord as an infant. He grew up serving in the tabernacle and became a prophet, priest, and judge for Israel. Samuel anointed Israel's first two kings, Saul and David.

1 Sam. 1:1–28; 3:1–21; 7:15–17; 10:1; 16:1–13

SANBALLAT AND TOBIAH

Sanballat was governor of Samaria during the time of Nehemiah. Tobiah was an important Ammonite official. Sanballat, Tobiah, and many others threatened Nehemiah because he was rebuilding the wall around Jerusalem. They did not want the Jews to reclaim Jerusalem. To protect his fellow workers, Nehemiah posted armed guards near the wall. He also encouraged them to courageously keep up the work. Nehemiah's efforts proved successful, and the wall was finished. Sanballat, Tobiah, and all of Judah's enemies were frightened and humbled. They realized God had helped Nehemiah accomplish this great task.

Neh. 2:1–20; 4:1–23; 6:1–19

SANHEDRIN

The Sanhedrin was a powerful ruling council for the Jewish people. It was made up of seventy members. The Sanhedrin functioned like a Supreme Court in religious matters. The high priest can be likened to a chief justice.

Matt. 26:57–66; John 11:47–53; Acts 4:13–15

SARAH

Sarah was the wife of Abraham, the founding father of the Israelites. God promised Abraham he would have many descendants. When Sarah was ninety, she miraculously gave birth to Isaac. Isaac grew up and had a son named Jacob. Jacob had twelve sons who became the nation of Israel. Through Sarah, God's amazing promise to Abraham was fulfilled.

Gen. 18:10–15; 21:1–13

SATAN

The word *satan* means "adversary." It is also the name of God's adversary the devil. Satan is the chief of demons. He violently opposes the plans, purposes, and people of God. Satan was originally a powerful, beautiful angel created by God. He became jealous of God's supreme power and rebelled. God cast Satan out of heaven, as well as the angels who had sided with him. Satan disguised himself as the serpent in the garden of Eden, where he deceived Eve and convinced her to disobey God's command. She ate fruit from the Tree of the Knowledge of Good and Evil and convinced Adam to eat it as well. As a result, sin and death entered the world. When Jesus began his ministry, God allowed Satan to tempt Jesus in the wilderness. Jesus stayed faithful to God and did not sin. Jesus later called Satan a murderer and liar and the prince of this world. In the book of Revelation, the devil is called "destroyer," "the dragon," "the serpent," and "the accuser." God will eventually destroy Satan in a lake of fire.

Isa. 14:12–15; Ezek. 28:12–19; Matt. 4:1–10; Luke 4:1–13; 10:18; John 8:44; Rev. 9:11; 12:9–13; 20:1–3

SAUL, KING

Saul was Israel's first king. God chose him because the Israelites wanted a king like other nations. Tall and handsome, Saul was from the tribe of Benjamin. Sadly, it wasn't long before he ignored God's instructions. God removed his Spirit from Saul and decided to make David king instead. Yet David waited on God's timing to take the throne. Saul grew jealous of David's military victories and spent years trying to kill him. During a battle with the Philistines, Saul was badly wounded and fell on his sword so he would quickly die.

1 Sam. 8:1–10:1; 13:1–14; 16:1–13; 18:1–15; 19:1–2; 31:1–6

SENNACHERIB

Sennacherib was an Assyrian king. When Assyria controlled the kingdom of Judah, King Hezekiah rebelled. Sennacherib responded by invading many cities in Judah. The prophet Isaiah encouraged Hezekiah by prophesying that Sennacherib would be defeated. Isaiah's word came to pass when the angel of the Lord killed 185,000 Assyrian troops.

2 Kings 18:7–19:37

SETH

Seth was Adam and Eve's third son. His name means "granted," since God granted Eve another child after her oldest son killed her youngest son. Seth's family line includes Noah, Abraham, Jacob, and Jesus Christ.

Gen. 4:25–5:3; Luke 3:23–38

SHADRACH, MESHACH, AND ABEDNEGO

These three young Jewish men were exiled to Babylon. They studied for service in the king's court alongside the prophet Daniel. Shadrach, Meshach, and Abednego had favor with the king until they refused to bow to one of his idols. The king said he would throw them into a blazing furnace unless they obeyed. But Shadrach, Meshach, and Abednego stayed faithful to God. When they were thrown into the furnace, they suffered no harm. God had sent his angel to protect them. The king was amazed and praised God. He even gave Shadrach, Meshach, and Abednego a promotion.

Dan. 1:1–20; 3:1–30

SHEBA

Sheba led the northern tribes of Israel in a rebellion against King David. David sent his army to fight Sheba. They began to destroy the wall of the town where Sheba had fled. To save her town, a wise woman reasoned with David's general. He agreed to stop their attack if the townspeople would hand over Sheba. The wise woman partnered with her fellow citizens, and they found Sheba and killed him.

2 Sam. 20:1–22

SHEM, HAM, AND JAPHETH

Shem, Ham, and Japheth were Noah's sons. After the flood, Noah planted a vineyard and enjoyed wine made from its grapes. But one day he drank too much and lay naked in his tent. Ham discovered that Noah was naked and told his brothers. Shem and Japheth covered their father's nakedness with a garment. After this, Noah prophesied that Ham's son Canaan would serve his brothers. Many years later, descendants of Shem—the Israelites—conquered the land of Canaan.

Gen. 5:32; 6:17–18; 9:20–27; 11:10–26; Ex. 19:5–6; Deut. 20:17–18

SHIMEI

Shimei was a relative of Saul's. When King David left Jerusalem to flee his son's rebellion, Shimei threw terrible insults upon David. Yet David did not harm Shimei. When David returned to reestablish his throne, Shimei begged for mercy. David promised Shimei would not die, but he asked his son Solomon to deal justly with him. When Solomon became king, he ordered that Shimei not leave Jerusalem. But when Shimei's slaves escaped, Shimei left to pursue them. Solomon put Shimei to death for this and for what he did to David.

2 Sam. 16:5–14; 1 Kings 2:8–9; 36–46

SILAS (SILVANUS)

Silas was a leader in the early Jerusalem church. He was also known by his Latin name, Silvanus. Silas went with the apostle Paul on his second missionary journey. Both he and Paul were arrested and beaten in Philippi. While in prison, they prayed and sang hymns until an earthquake shook open the doors. Paul and Silas shared the gospel with the jailer who was guarding them. He believed the gospel and was baptized. Silas played an important role helping Paul serve the new churches they established.

Acts 15:22; 16:25–34; 18:5; 2 Cor. 1:19

SIMEON, JACOB'S SON

Jacob and his wife Leah named their second son Simeon. Simeon, with his brother Levi, killed the residents of Shechem to avenge their sister's rape. When Simeon went with his brothers to buy grain in Egypt, Joseph held him as a ransom until his brothers returned with Benjamin.

Gen. 29:33; 34:1–26; 42:1–43:23

SIMEON

Simeon was an older Jewish man who faithfully waited for Israel's restoration. God had promised Simeon he would not die until he saw Israel's Messiah. God kept his promise and led Simeon to the temple on the same day Mary and Joseph dedicated the infant Jesus. The old man rejoiced in getting to see the Messiah and prophesied over Jesus and Mary. Simeon said Jesus would suffer to bring salvation to all people. He also told Mary that she, too, would share a part in his suffering.

Luke 2:25–35

SIMON OF CYRENE

As Jesus was led away to Golgotha, Simon of Cyrene was passing through Jerusalem. The Romans seized him and forced him to carry Jesus's cross. Mark identifies him as the

father of Alexander and Rufus. Possibly this is the same
Rufus mentioned in Romans 16:13.

Mark 15:21–22

SIMON THE ZEALOT

Simon was the disciple of Jesus described as a zealot. He
may have been a member of the Zealots—a revolutionary
political group that wanted to drive the Romans out of the
Jewish homeland. Or he was simply a religious zealot and
cared very deeply about God's law.

Matt. 10:2–4

SOLOMON, KING

King Solomon was a son of King David and his wife
Bathsheba. Solomon ruled over Israel during its time of
greatest glory. He built Israel's first temple—a holy place
to worship God in Jerusalem. Solomon is
famous for his wisdom. He is the author
of the books of Proverbs, Ecclesiastes,
and Song of Songs. Later in life,
however, he foolishly took
seven hundred foreign
wives and three hundred
concubines. They led
him to worship
false gods. This
grieved God's heart, so
he tore the kingdom from
Solomon's son Rehoboam.

The result was that Israel was divided into a northern and southern kingdom.

2 Sam. 12:24–25; 1 Kings 3:1–14; 11:1–12:24; 1 Chron. 22:1–23:1

STEPHEN

Stephen was part of a group that helped care for widows in the Jerusalem church. Filled with the Holy Spirit, Stephen performed miracles in the name of Jesus. Some of the Jewish people opposed him and falsely accused him of breaking God's law. They violently seized him and brought him before the Jewish religious leaders. Stephen responded by accusing them of being stubborn like so many of their ancestors had been. The Jewish leaders were furious and stoned Stephen to death.

Acts 6:1–8:2

TABITHA (DORCAS)

Tabitha was a disciple known for sewing clothes for those in need and giving to the poor. When she died of an illness, the apostle Peter raised her from the dead.

Acts 9:36–42

TAMAR, JUDAH'S DAUGHTER-IN-LAW

Tamar was the daughter-in-law of Judah. When Judah's oldest son died, she married Judah's middle son. When he also died, Judah promised Tamar she would marry his third son after he grew up. As time passed, Tamar realized that Judah was not going to follow through. She disguised herself as a prostitute and waited by the road. When Judah came along, she slept with him so she could have a child. Tamar gave birth to twin sons: Perez and Zerah. Perez is an ancestor of Jesus.

Gen. 38:6–30; Matt. 1:1–16

TAMAR, DAVID'S DAUGHTER

Tamar was a daughter of King David. Her half-brother Amnon lusted after her beauty. When she refused to sleep with him, he raped her. Afterward he rejected her and sent her away. Disgraced, she remained unmarried and lived with her brother Absalom.

2 Sam. 13:1–20

THADDAEUS

Thaddaeus is listed among the original disciples. Some scholars think Thaddaeus is another name for Judas the son of James (Luke 6:16; Acts 1:13). If so, he asked this question of Jesus: "Lord, why do you intend to show yourself to us and not to the world?" (John 14:22). Nothing further is known about him.

Matt. 10:1–3

THEOPHILUS

Luke addressed his gospel and the book of Acts to Theophilus. Very little is known about Theophilus, but he seems to have been a person of high social standing. Luke addressed him as "most excellent" at the beginning of his gospel. Theophilus may have been a wealthy man who financed Luke's writing.

Luke 1:3; Acts 1:1

THOMAS

Thomas was one of the twelve disciples. He was also called Didymus, which means "the twin." Thomas is remembered as the "doubting disciple" because he doubted the other disciples who said they had seen the risen Jesus. A week later, Jesus appeared to the disciples again when Thomas was with them. Thomas's doubt disappeared as he worshiped at Jesus's feet.

Mark 3:13–18; John 20:19–29

TIBERIUS CAESAR

Tiberius was the Roman emperor during the ministry of Jesus. Tiberius appointed Pontius Pilate as the governor of Judea. When Pilate tried to free Jesus, the Jewish leaders claimed that Pilate was "no friend of Caesar [Tiberius]."

Luke 3:1–2; John 19:12

TIMOTHY

Timothy was a devoted Christian and a trusted coworker of the apostle Paul. He went with Paul on Paul's second missionary journey. When Timothy became a pastor in the Ephesus church, Paul wrote the letters of 1 and 2 Timothy to encourage him. Timothy also delivered many of Paul's letters to various churches. In those letters, Paul often referred to Timothy's valuable help or included his name as a coauthor. Like Paul, Timothy was imprisoned at one time because of his faith.

Acts 16:1–5; 19:21–22; Rom. 16:21; 1 Cor. 4:17; 1 Tim. 1:1–4

TITUS

Titus was one of the apostle Paul's most faithful and trusted coworkers. Paul took Titus with him to preach the gospel on the island of Crete. Titus stayed and became a pastor there. Later Paul wrote a letter of instruction and encouragement to Titus as he oversaw that church. Today this letter is known as the New Testament book of Titus.

2 Cor. 2:12–13; 7:6–7; Gal. 2:1–3; Titus 1:4–5

URIAH THE HITTITE

Uriah was one of "the Thirty" famous soldiers in King David's army. He was also Bathsheba's husband. While

Uriah was faithfully battling the Ammonites, David arranged for Uriah's death to cover up that he had committed adultery with Bathsheba.

2 Sam. 11:1–17; 23:24, 39

UZZIAH (AZARIAH), KING

Uzziah became Judah's tenth king at age sixteen. He followed God in many ways and had a long and prosperous reign. But when he violated God's law by performing priestly duties, God struck him with a skin disease until the day he died.

2 Kings 14:21–22; 15:1–7; 2 Chron. 26:1–23

VASHTI, QUEEN

When King Xerxes of Persia demanded that Vashti display her beauty at a banquet, Vashti refused to come. The king's advisers removed her as queen, so Xerxes chose Esther, a beautiful young Jewish girl, as his next queen.

Est. 1:1–19; 2:17; 7:1–8:11

ZACCHAEUS

Zacchaeus was once a corrupt tax collector in Jericho. But Zacchaeus's life was changed one day after he climbed a tree to catch a glimpse of Jesus. Jesus saw him and told Zacchaeus to come down so he could stay at

Zacchaeus's house. Zacchaeus was overjoyed. He promised Jesus he would repay four times the money he had stolen from others. He also promised to give half of what he owned to the poor.

Luke 19:1–10

ZADOK THE HIGH PRIEST

Zadok the priest was a famous descendant of Aaron, Israel's first high priest. Zadok served in the tabernacle during the time of King David. He was loyal to David when two of David's sons tried to take David's throne. Zadok also became Solomon's chief priest. Much later, God proclaimed that only Zadok's descendants could serve inside the temple since the Levites had allowed idol worship.

2 Sam. 15:24; 20:25; 1 Kings 1:8;
Ezek. 44:10–16

ZEBULUN

Zebulun was the tenth son of Jacob and the youngest son of Leah. Because Leah had already given Jacob several sons, she hoped that Jacob would treat her with honor after Zebulun's birth.

Gen. 30:19–20

ZECHARIAH, FATHER OF JOHN THE BAPTIST

Zechariah, a Jewish priest, was on duty in the temple when he was visited by an angel. The angel told Zechariah that his prayers had been heard. His wife, Elizabeth, would give birth to a son. This was surprising since Zechariah and Elizabeth were elderly and childless. The angel told Zechariah to name their son John. He would prepare the Jewish people for the coming of the Messiah. When Zechariah doubted this, he was unable to speak. After the birth of his son, Zechariah wrote a message that the boy's name was to be John. Suddenly he could speak again. At that moment, Zechariah praised God and spoke about how John would play a special role in God's plan of salvation.

Luke 1:5–25, 57–79

ZECHARIAH THE PROPHET

Zechariah was a prophet when the Jewish exiles were returning to Judah. Zechariah encouraged the people of Judah to return to God and continue rebuilding the demolished temple. His message was that God would bring about good things for Judah and Jerusalem. He also spoke about a day when all people—Jews and Gentiles—would come to Jerusalem to worship the Lord.

Ezra 5:1–2; Zech. 1:1; 8:14–23; 14:17

ZEDEKIAH, KING

Zedekiah was the final king of Judah. He was taken captive to Babylon, where he watched the officials kill his sons before gouging out his eyes. The Babylonians destroyed the temple in Jerusalem and sent the people of Judah into exile.

2 Kings 24:17–25:7; 2 Chron. 36:10–13

ZEPHANIAH

Before Babylon destroyed Jerusalem, Zephaniah the prophet told the people of Judah about God's coming judgment. He called it "the day of the LORD" and warned it would be terrible for Judah, its neighboring nations, and everyone who worshiped false gods. Zephaniah called Judah to turn back to the Lord. He promised that God would raise up people who would be faithful to him and live safely in Jerusalem.

Zeph. 1:1–6; 2:1–3; 3:11–13

ZERUBBABEL

Zerubbabel helped lead the first group of Jewish exiles back to Jerusalem. Under Zerubbabel's leadership, the temple was rebuilt after the Babylonians destroyed it. He also served as the governor of Judah during this time. Zerubbabel is listed as an ancestor of Jesus Christ.

Ezra 1:2–4; 2:1–2; Hag. 1:1; Matt. 1:1, 12–13

ZIBA

Ziba was a servant of King Saul. When David was king, he told Ziba he wanted to show kindness to Saul's descendants. Ziba told David about Mephibosheth, Saul's grandson. David started to care for Mephibosheth and ordered that Ziba be Mephibosheth's servant. Later Ziba told David that Mephibosheth had betrayed David. But Mephibosheth claimed that Ziba lied. David made peace by giving Mephibosheth and Ziba equal portions of land.

2 Sam. 9:1–13; 16:1–4; 19:24–30

ZIPPORAH

Zipporah was the wife of Moses. To obey God's command, she circumcised their firstborn son. After Moses led the Israelites out of Egypt, Zipporah and her family traveled to join Moses in the desert.

Ex. 2:15–22; 4:21–25; 18:1–6

MADE EASY

by Rose Publishing

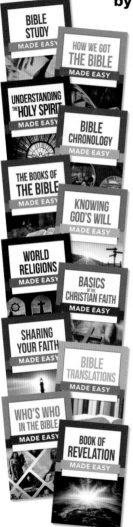

BIBLE STUDY
A step-by-step guide to studying God's Word

HOW WE GOT THE BIBLE
Key events in the history of the Bible

UNDERSTANDING THE HOLY SPIRIT
Who the Holy Spirit is and what he does

BIBLE CHRONOLOGY
Bible events in the order they happened

THE BOOKS OF THE BIBLE
Quick summaries of all 66 books of the Bible

KNOWING GOD'S WILL
Answers to tough questions about God's will

WORLD RELIGIONS
30 religions and how they compare to Christianity

BASICS OF THE CHRISTIAN FAITH
Key Christian beliefs and practices

SHARING YOUR FAITH
How to share the gospel

BIBLE TRANSLATIONS
Compares 20 popular Bible versions

BOOK OF REVELATION
Who, what, where, when, and why of Revelation

WHO'S WHO IN THE BIBLE
Key facts about the Bible's main characters

www.hendricksonrose.com